Editor
Lorin E. Klistoff, M.A.

Managing Editor
Karen Goldfluss, M.S. Ed.

Editor-in-Chief
Sharon Coan, M.S. Ed.

Illustrator
Sue Fullam

Cover Artist
Brenda DiAntonis

Art Coordinator
Kevin Barnes

Art Director
CJae Froshay

Imaging
Ralph Olmedo, Jr.

Product Manager
Phil Garcia

Publishers
Rachelle Cracchiolo, M.S. Ed.
Mary Dupuy Smith, M.S. Ed.

CREATIVE Writing

Primary

The Mystery of the Carrot Thief

Compiled by

J.L. Smith, M.A.

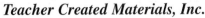

Teacher Created Materials

Teacher Created Materials, Inc.
6421 Industry Way
Westminster, CA 92683
www.teachercreated.com.

ISBN-0-7439-3274-9

©2002 Teacher Created Materials, Inc.

Made in U.S.A.

Table of Contents

Introduction

This book is designed to promote creative writing in your classroom. The contents provide ideas—beginning with the planning stages all the way through final publishing—to help your students become very creative writers.

The first section, *Getting Creative*, provides everything your students will need in the pre-writing stage to plan out their story. Included are ideas to stimulate pre-writing, templates for story maps, and checklists to help students make sure they have remembered to plan for all the components of a story.

If you need ideas for putting together a story, the section titled *Creative Story Writing* will give you plot ideas for the beginning, middle, and ending of a story, as well as ideas for settings and characters.

Try some of the ideas in *Creative Ideas for Creative Writing* to help your students come up with their own creative writing ideas and topics. In this section are a variety of ways to get students thinking creatively so that they can then apply their ideas in a story.

If you would still like to provide additional creative support to your students, try some of the ideas in the section called *Prompting Creativity*. This section provides creative and fun ways to get students thinking about a variety of writing topics. The projects provide a fun way to capture your students' attention and prompt their creative writing.

Finally, the section titled *Creative Publishing* provides a variety of different ways to publish your creative writing masterpiece. Included are ideas for creative publishing, such as patterns for making books and stationery.

Pre-writing Activities

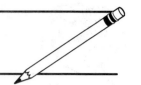

In order to write, you must have something to write about. The lack of ideas stops many would-be-writers from ever starting. They find it frustrating to be told to write when they have no idea where to begin.

Pre-writing activities help formulate ideas before writing begins. It is a brainstorming stage, one that leads to a fluency of thoughts that can produce an idea which the students may want to capture on paper. This step in the writing process builds self-confidence and self-esteem, as well as helps to create the motivation necessary to write. Pre-writing also serves as an organizational tool, guiding the students in their writing plan.

There are many ways to stimulate pre-writing. Here are just a few. Deposit your ideas for writing in the word and idea bank on page 6.

Reading: Read literature—including stories, poems, plays, newspapers, cereal boxes, magazines, T-shirts, maps, logs, journals, diaries, and classroom walls!

Listening: Listen to literature—instrumental and vocal music, sounds in nature, TV, radio, videos, films, and commercials.

Smelling: Smell things—food cooking, flowers, types of herbs and spices, dirty socks, and the outdoors.

Tasting: Taste specific foods with different types of herbs and spices, sweets, sours, and bitters.

Observing: Look at photographs, colors, pictures, posters, objects, nature, doodles, and each other.

Touching: Touch different textures, different hands, and different temperatures.

Doing: Experience role playing skits, field trips, classroom guests, and creative dramatics.

A Storm in Your Brain!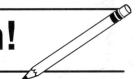

When you start thinking of ideas, you are brainstorming. When you brainstorm, don't stop to think about whether your ideas are good or not, just write them all down. You can brainstorm alone or with others. To try brainstorming alone, pick one of the ideas from the list below. Write the idea in the circle. Then, think of everything and anything that comes to your mind about this topic. Write everything you think of in the box around the circle. Don't worry if some of your ideas seem silly or not "correct." Just write down everything, and don't stop until you are sure you have run out of ideas.

- candy
- yellow things
- summer

- my grandma
- merry-go-rounds
- sports

- food
- sticky things
- pets

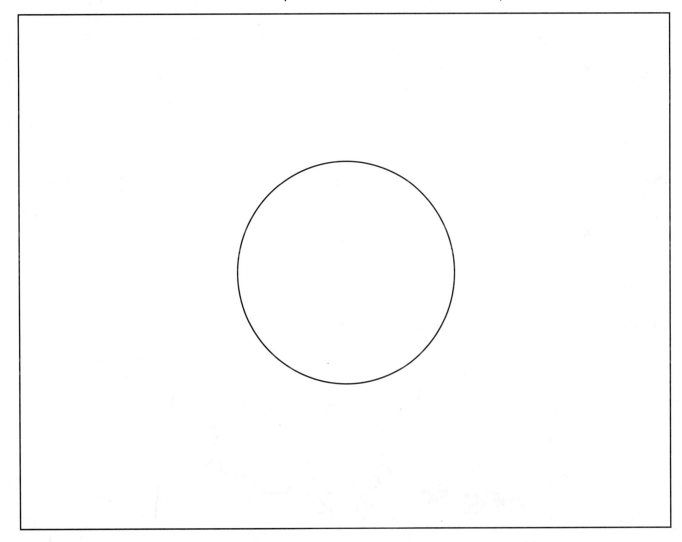

Challenge: After you have finished brainstorming, circle the ideas you like best, and write a story using your topic and your ideas.

Word and Idea Bank

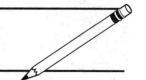

Collect all the words or ideas you can on a specific subject and "deposit" them in the "bank" below.

Topic: _____

Story Map I

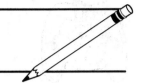

Directions: Use this map to help you plan the different parts of your story.

Setting (where and when)

Character(s)

Conflict

Action/Events

Resolution

Story Map II

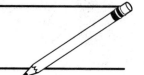

Directions: Use this map to help you plan the different parts of your story.

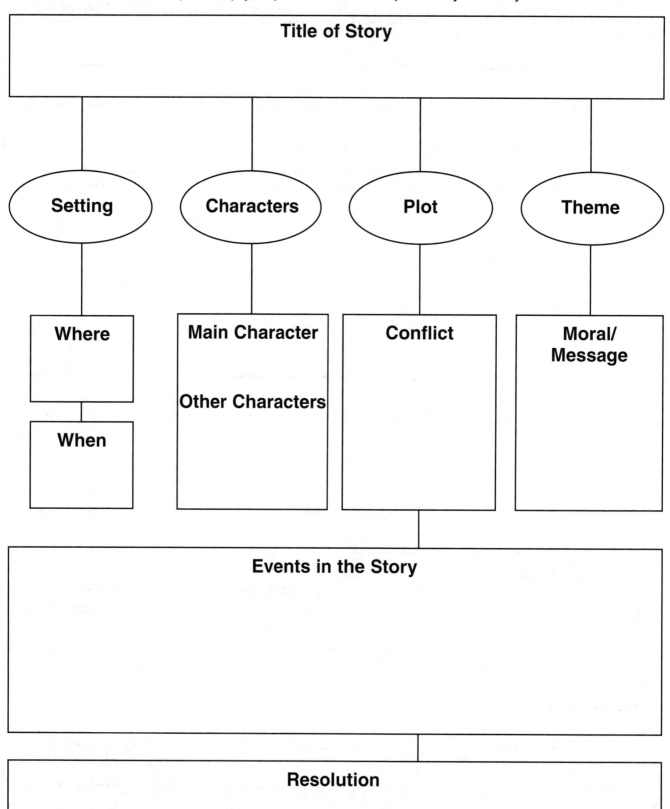

Title of Story

Setting   Characters   Plot   Theme

Where

When

Main Character

Other Characters

Conflict

Moral/
Message

Events in the Story

Resolution

8

Story Web

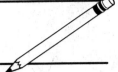

WHO
is in the story?

WHY
do the events take place?

WHAT
happens in the story?

_____

_____

_____

_____

_____

_____   _____   _____

_____   _____   _____

_____   _____   _____

_____   _____   _____

Title: _____

WHEN
do the events happen?

HOW does the story end?
(How are the problems
resolved?)

WHERE
does the story take place?

_____   _____   _____

_____   _____   _____

_____   _____   _____

_____   _____   _____

Story Summary

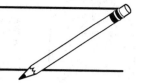

Use the brainstorming sheet below to help you plan out the main elements of your story. Use this as a guide while you are writing your story.

Beginning

Who (is the main character)? _____

Where (will the story take place)? _____

When (does this story happen)? _____

What (happens during the beginning of the story)? _____

Why or how (does the action take place)? _____

Middle

Who (are the main characters in this part of the story)? _____

Where (is this part of the story taking place)? _____

When (does it take place—after that, after awhile, the next day, etc.)?

_____

What (are the main things that happen in this part of the story)?

_____

Why or how (does the action take place)? _____

End

Who (are the main characters in this part of the story)? _____

Where (is this part of the story taking place)? _____

When (does it happen—after awhile, suddenly, two weeks later)? _____

What (happens in this section of the story)? _____

Why or how (is the problem solved)? _____

First, Next, Then, Finally

Use this pre-writing form to help you plan out the sequence of events in your story.

First, _____

_____

_____

_____

_____

_____

_____

_____

_____

_____

Next, _____

_____

_____

_____

_____

_____

_____

_____

_____

_____

Then, _____

_____

_____

_____

_____

_____

_____

_____

_____

_____

Finally, _____

_____

_____

_____

_____

_____

_____

_____

_____

_____

Writing a Comedy

Characters

Setting

Conflict

Resolution to the
Conflict

Funny part(s) of the
Story

Illustrate what happens in your funny story in the cartoon frames below.

How to Write an Innovation

Innovations can be created from poems, stories, or books by substituting nouns, verbs, and adjectives to fit a new context. For example, if the original story is set in the jungle, an innovation could be written about the oceans. Different animal names and descriptive words would be substituted to reflect the new setting. Model the process with students until they become comfortable with it and can write one on their own or with minimal supervision.

Step by Step Directions

1. As a whole group, decide on one story to innovate. (For the purposes of this example, *The Great Kapok Tree* will be used.)

2. Discuss the setting of the story (the Amazon rain forest). Once the setting has been established, brainstorm other settings. Vote on one to use for the innovation. (For the purposes of this example, the ocean will be used.)

3. Brainstorm lists of ocean words—animals, plants, sounds, descriptive words and phrases, etc. Use these words to replace specified words in the text.

4. Write the sentences in correct sequence on the chalkboard or overhead projector.

5. Rehearse innovations of the title: "The Gigantic Kelp Bed." One sentence at a time, make changes in each sentence. For example, "The **boa** told how the **tree** was his home." Changing the bolded nouns might produce, "The **otter** told how the **kelp bed** was his home." Continue until all lines have been changed.

6. Divide the students into groups and assign them a specific amount of text. You can write the text for them or they may copy the text themselves onto a sheet of paper. Direct them to illustrate their text. Compile the pages to make a big book or display the pages on the walls.

The Gigantic Kelp Bed
by
Keith   Joe   Kim
Tom Dennis Jennifer

The otter told how the kelp bed was his home.

The sea urchin told how he gets his food from the kelp bed.

Innovation Story Map

	Original	Innovation
Title		
Setting		
Characters		
Events		
Words Important to the Story (descriptive words and phrases)		

Writing Tall Tales

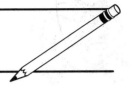

A **tall tale** is a story based on fact, but told in a highly exaggerated and humorous way. Define exaggeration for your class as something that goes beyond the truth. Read a variety of tall tales to your class. How do they go "beyond the truth?" Have students discuss what makes each a tall tale. List the reasons on a chart entitled "Tall Tale Exaggerations."

Give students an opportunity to write a tall tale. To help them organize their thoughts, either use the Tall Tale Story Map on page 16 or have students fold their papers into three columns. They should then label the columns "Character," "Setting," and "Exaggeration." Direct them to fill in the columns by using either their own ideas or the information on the class Tall Tale Exaggerations chart. Then, using this new chart they have made, have each of them write a story. Children may draw a picture to illustrate their story.

Some ideas for stories include the following:

- The Day the Rain Fell Up Instead of Down

- My Speedy Fast Turtle

- I Woke Up in a Cartoon

- My Wild Pet, Tornado Tilly

- The Day I Had Spaghetti for Hair

- A Tornado Drank Up the Wind

- The Day I Flew to School

- The Day We Had No Weather

A fun way to publish a tall tale is on a long strip of cashier tape or other long piece of paper. In this way, the story can be tall both literally and in the story.

Tall Tale Story Map

Setting (where and when)

Character(s)

Exaggeration(s)

Conflict

Solution

Different Ways of Seeing

Try rewriting one of these fairy tales from a different point of view.

The Gingerbread Man from the point of view of the fox.

The Three Little Pigs from the point of view of the wolf.

Goldilocks from the point of view of the baby bear.

Little Red Riding Hood from the point of view of the grandmother.

The Three Billy Goats Gruff from the point of view of the troll.

Rapunzel from the point of view of Rumplestilskin.

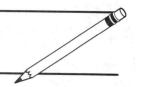

Writing Ideas

The following is a list of areas where writing is used. Ask the students to brainstorm a similar list for themselves. See who can come up with the most ideas. Use this list to help you create a variety of writing assignments.

- postcards
- menus
- mottoes
- letters
- daily bulletins/news
- billboards
- invitations
- jokes
- drivers' licenses
- cartoons
- riddles
- name tags
- newspaper articles
- bumper stickers
- greeting cards
- newspaper ads
- questions
- thank-you notes
- flyers
- recipes
- imaginary characters

- pop-up books
- directions
- imaginary objects
- sentence frames
- story summaries
- magazine covers
- word lists
- poetry
- announcements
- calendars
- notes
- schedules
- phone messages
- reminder notes
- lists
- "for sale" signs
- brainstorming
- "help wanted" ads
- autobiographies
- greeting cards
- resumés

- graphic organizers
- fairy tales
- family histories
- story mapping
- character descriptions
- folk tales
- gift tags
- commercials
- letterheads
- addresses on envelopes
- labels
- business cards
- weather reports
- ID cards
- wanted posters
- diaries
- conversation hearts
- captions for photos or post cards
- license plates

Writer's Checklist

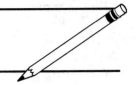

When you have a final copy, it's time for one last check. Before you turn in your story, use this checklist to be sure it is ready.

_____ Did you include a setting in your story?

_____ Is there a problem for your main character in your story?

_____ Does your main character (protagonist) seem like he or she is real?

_____ Is your story interesting?

_____ Have you used any of the five senses in your story?

_____ Did you remember to "show" and not "tell"?

_____ Have you checked the spelling and grammar?

_____ Have you read the story aloud to be sure that it makes sense?

What Is a Story?

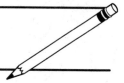

A **story** is a tale. It can be long or it can be told or it can be written. A story can be short or it can be long. A story that is very long is called a novel. A story can be true (nonfiction) or made up (fiction).

Real or true stories (nonfiction) can be found in magazines or books, and they can be in the form of biographies (stories about people) or true adventures.

Realistic stories (fiction) are stories that tell about someone or something, and they seem real. They can be found in historical and adventure novels.

Fantasy stories (fiction) are stories about characters and places that are not like anyone or anyplace you have ever known. These would include tall tales, fairy tales, science fiction, and of course stories about talking animals that do amazing things!

A story is a work of art that has been carefully planned by the author. You know when you read a good story. It makes you think, learn, laugh, cry, feel glad, feel sad, feel afraid, or just feel really good.

You have probably already written and told many stories. A story usually has the following parts:

- a beginning, a middle, and an ending

- two or three characters, but sometimes more

- descriptions of the characters and the setting

- use of the five senses

- expressions of feelings

- dialogue

- a problem

- a solution for the problem

Story Wheel

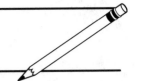

Cut out the story wheel. Use a paper clip as a spinner. Take a pencil and use the tip to hold the paper clip at the center of the wheel. Give each student a chance to spin the paper clip. When the paper clip stops, that is the type of story that the student will write. Spend time in class sharing your stories.

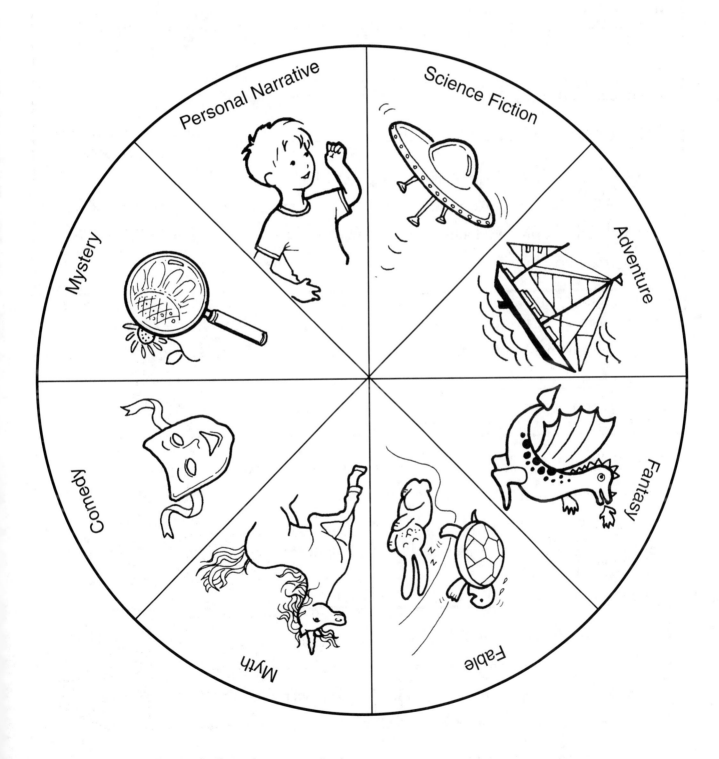

Personal Narrative

Science Fiction

Adventure

Fantasy

Fable

Myth

Comedy

Mystery

Off to a Good Beginning

All stories have a beginning, a middle, and an ending. Cut out these story starters and place them in a small container or envelope. Select a story starter out of the container to be the beginning of your story. Try using the same story starter more than once and write a different story each time. Write some more story starters to add to these.

Lindsay was so happy with her new puppy. She named him "Pookie," and she was teaching him to shake hands and roll over. He was just a fluffy ball of fur, and he liked to give her doggie kisses all over her face. She hurried home from school each day to play with Pookie, but one day the puppy wasn't there.

My mom told me to take a box of cookies to my grandma's house around the corner. I put them in the basket of my bicycle and started pedaling. As soon as I got to the end of the street, I saw the Dawson brothers, the neighborhood bullies, standing there with their arms folded and looking really mean.

David walked home from school very slowly. His friends were laughing and running around, but David just kept walking. He watched his toes step onto the sidewalk over and over again. When he finally got home, he trudged up the front porch steps, and there stood his mother watching him. "What's wrong with you?" she asked.

Our neighbors' tree grew so big that it came right over our fence. One day I was looking at it and decided that I could climb it. I grabbed the lowest branch and pulled myself up to the trunk and then kept climbing until I got to the top. You wouldn't believe what I saw!

Stuck in the Middle

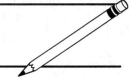

You will have to be very creative for this challenge. Try to incorporate these writing scenarios in the middle of your story. You will have to come up with a beginning and an ending to your story that makes the story flow.

Sam shouted loudly so that I could hear. He yelled that he thought I was a chicken for not wanting to go into the haunted house. Sam went in and began climbing up the broken staircase. I came to the doorway and said I thought the stairs were going to break. Sam said I was just afraid of stairs, ghosts, and haunted houses. Then Karen came up and tried to get me to go in. She said that she would go with me so that Sam wouldn't think I was a chicken. I decided not to go in. Karen went on in to follow Sam. I sat and waited for over half an hour. Suddenly, . . .

Now, they were miles from nowhere. The sun was starting to set, and Martha suggested that they head back. Kathryn agreed that it was a good idea. The girls looked around for some trail markers. They couldn't find any. "Oh, no!" said Martha, "We're lost, and we don't even have a flashlight!"

Kristen ran into the stable and threw her arms around Ginger. Ginger was Kristen's very own horse. "They can't sell you," sobbed Kristen. She clung to Ginger's mane and stroked it gently. She cried over and over again. All of a sudden, she jumped on Ginger's back, and they raced out of the stable.

When Emily walked in the house, she could hear her mom talking on the phone. She was talking to Mrs. March, Emily's teacher! What could this mean? Emily's mom yelled, "Emily, it's for you!"

The snake came slithering out of its cage. Not one of the students in Mr. Schmidt's class even noticed. Soon after the snake slithered off the counter, the lunch bell rang.

In the End

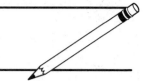

Select one of the cards from below to use as the ending for your story. You will have to write the beginning and middle of your story so that the end fits with the story.

When she gets to her grandmother's house, she discovers that it's not her grandmother at all, but the wolf! A woodsman hears them, comes to rescue her, and lets her grandmother out of the closet where she has been hiding, safe and sound.

She waits so long that she is certain she will never have a piano. Then one day, she receives a letter from her grandmother, saying that she is not using her piano anymore and will gladly trade it for a lap blanket and wonders if Elise can knit one in blue for her.

When his family finally goes to the airport, they are surprised to see so many airport travelers saying "hi" to Timmy. They are also surprised when Timmy walks on board with a smile on his face. When they wave good-bye to grandpa, they wonder why he is winking at Timmy.

One day, she comes home and finds the entire room cleaned up by her sister. There is one little mess on the floor where her sister is putting all of her stickers into a scrapbook.

The next day at school he tells Tran that he really likes his book report and asks if he would like to play kickball with him. Tran is glad that he has a friend, and soon Daniel makes many more friends.

She practices so much that when she gets up in front of her class, she is only a little bit nervous at first, and soon it is easy. When she finishes, she sighs and smiles.

What a Character!

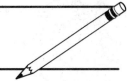

Cut out the characters below and mix them up. Put the choices in a hat or box and choose, without looking, two characters. Write a story using the characters you have selected. If you need an idea for a setting, see page 28.

a babysitter	a puppy	a stuffed animal
a teacher	a dad	a monster
an artist	a clown	a nurse
a mom	a fireman	a child
a kitten	the newspaper boy	the president
a police man	a grandma	a doctor
a baby	a ghost	the mayor
a waitress	the principal	a minister
a bear	a teenager	a dentist
a grandpa	a snake	a toy store worker
the librarian	a monkey	Santa Claus

Developing a Character

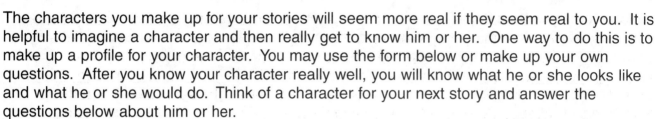

The characters you make up for your stories will seem more real if they seem real to you. It is helpful to imagine a character and then really get to know him or her. One way to do this is to make up a profile for your character. You may use the form below or make up your own questions. After you know your character really well, you will know what he or she looks like and what he or she would do. Think of a character for your next story and answer the questions below about him or her.

Name of Character_____

Age_____ Height_____ Weight_____ Male or Female _____

Hair Color _____ Eye Color _____ Skin Color _____

Where does he or she live? _____

What does he or she do each day (job, school, etc.)? _____

List the character's favorite: Color _____ Hobby _____

Food _____ Sport _____

Animal _____ Music _____ Book _____

Place to go _____ Movie _____

Thing to do on a rainy day _____

Thing to do on a sunny day _____

Best friend_____ Worst enemy _____

Personality (funny, serious, shy, bold, etc.) _____

Would you like to have this character as a friend? _____

Why or why not? _____

All Set!

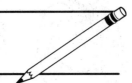

Have you ever seen a play on stage? If you have, you probably noticed there was a set on the stage even before the actors went on stage. The set may have been the inside of a house, an outdoor scene, or maybe even a circus. When you write a story, you need a set, too, for your characters. You won't need to build it with a hammer and nails, though. You will build it in your imagination and write it on paper. With stories, the set is called a **setting**. Sometimes it helps to write about your setting if you first draw what it looks like. Using a story that you want to write or a favorite story, draw a setting for it in the space below. Be sure to add color. Don't add the characters; only draw the setting.

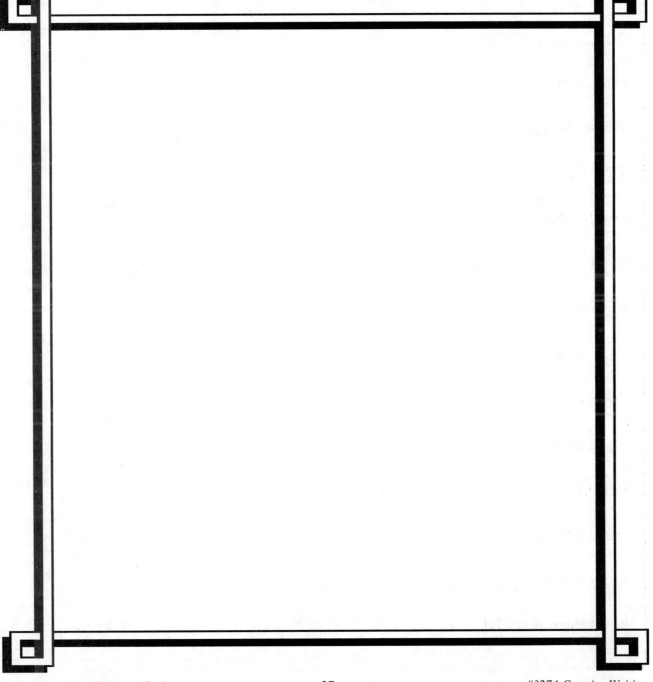

Setting the Stage

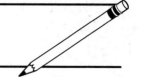

Cut out the settings below and mix them up. Put the choices in a hat or box and choose a setting. If you need ideas for characters, select two characters from the list on page 25.

the circus	a picnic	a baseball game
a playground	a store	a beach
a movie theater	the park	a birthday party
a dance	a rainstorm	a parade
a classroom	the library	the bus stop
a convenience store	the video arcade	an amusement park
a snowfall	the school lunchroom	a fast-food restaurant
a bakery	the seashore	a barn
the airport	the gas station	an ice cream parlor
a bowling alley	the zoo	a soccer game
a swimming pool	the hair salon/barber shop	a shoe store

All Mixed Up!

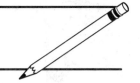

Choose one item from each group to use in a story. You can add other characters, settings, objects, and situations to your story.

A.
- ❏ a phone call
- ❏ a fight
- ❏ a letter
- ❏ an accident

B.
- ❏ a playground
- ❏ a birthday party
- ❏ a classroom
- ❏ a soccer field

C.
- ❏ a first grader
- ❏ a parent
- ❏ a doctor
- ❏ a teacher

D.
- ❏ an animal
- ❏ a backpack
- ❏ a rope
- ❏ a lunchbox

_____

_____

_____

_____

_____

_____

_____

_____

_____

_____

_____

_____

_____

_____

_____

_____

_____

Team Stories

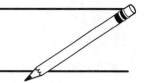

Have you ever made up stories with your friends with each of you taking a turn to add to the story? It can be fun to add your part to a story that is written by a team of writers.

Here is how to do it with your whole class:

1. Take out a piece of paper. Your teacher will give you some time to write a one-page or one-paragraph beginning to a story. Think of ways to make it interesting. Be sure to write about a character or two and a place for the characters. Will they be at school, on a mountain trail, on another planet, or at home? Be creative and think of the most interesting characters you can. Put the characters in a very interesting place. Add a title at the top of the story.

2. When you have finished, look carefully to make sure other people will be able to read what you wrote.

3. Your teacher will stop you when the time is up. Stop and turn in your story start.

4. After all the story starts are collected, your teacher will collect them and make copies.

5. Next, your teacher will pass out the story starts (maybe on another day). You should have one that someone else wrote. If you get your own, be sure to let your teacher know.

6. You will have time to write the middle part of someone else's story now. Be sure to use the same characters that are in the beginning of the story and decide how it will continue.

7. Check to make sure your middle can be read by others and turn it in. Your teacher will copy the new, longer stories.

8. Finally, it will be time to write the endings to the stories. Your teacher will pass out the stories again. Be sure that you get a story that was written by others and not you.

9. Now you have the tough job of writing an ending to a story that you did not start. Be sure to use the same characters and write an ending that makes sense.

10. Your teacher will collect all of the stories. Soon you will have a story festival, sharing the team stories.

Team Stories

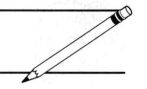

The Story Festival

Your teacher will state the title of the first story to be read. The author of the story's beginning will come up to read the whole story. When you hear the title you wrote, you will go to the front of the class to read your team's story. You may be surprised at what happened to your story. When you finish reading the whole story, you may tell the class how you thought the story would go and what surprised you about the middle and ending.

When everyone is finished, discuss the stories. Did anyone have trouble continuing a story? Why? Did any story come out just as expected? What were you thinking or feeling as you were writing your story parts? Which was the most fun: the beginning, the middle, or the ending? Which was the easiest to write?

Challenge: In a report folder with about ten pages, write a story start on the first page. Add your name to the bottom of the page. Put your folder in a box or on a shelf with the story folders of the rest of the class. When you have some free time, take out another folder, add a page to whatever story had been started, and add your name to the bottom of that page. Don't write your pages one after another; be sure to allow someone else a turn in between. You can write in as many books as you like. If you want, you can add an illustration to your page. Don't forget to read the stories too.

For Younger Students: Have the class, or a team of students, sit in a circle. Allot a time period, and pick a number so that students can try to guess the number. The student who comes closest gets to begin. The first student starts the story by introducing the characters and the setting, begins to tell some of the action, and then stops. The student to his or her left takes up where the first student left off and stops to allow the next student to continue, and so on. Continue as many times around the circle as time allows. (If you use a timer, let students see how much time is left, and it may motivate them to start tying together loose ends to create a conclusion.)

Team Stories

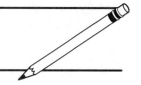

Here are some story starters to help you.

Tomas ran home from school as fast as he could. He wanted to watch his favorite show. When he got inside the house, his brother, Hector, was standing in front of the TV. "I think you better take care of something first," he said. "What?" Tomas asked, trying to get around his brother. "Go look at Rexie," Hector said. Tomas went into the backyard and whistled for his big white dog, Rexie. Rexie came running around the corner, but he wasn't white anymore. He was green!

When Megan woke up, she rubbed her eyes and stumbled into the kitchen to find something to eat. After she ate, she looked around the house. There was no radio on, no TV on, and her brother, Jeffery, was not taking a shower. It was really quiet. "Where is everybody?" she said.

After getting off the Ferris wheel, Kyle and Cori went to get some cotton candy. Their parents were going to meet them by the pony rides, where their little sister, Eliza, wanted to go for a ride. As they were getting their cotton candy, they argued about who should pay. Kyle owed Cori $2.00, and he hadn't paid her yet. They argued all the way to the pony rides. They stopped because they didn't want to go home yet. They looked around and didn't see their parents or Eliza anywhere. On a bench they found three packages, and they each had Cori's name on them.

Sara put her stuffed animals and dolls carefully on the shelf each night before she went to bed. Then her mom read her a bedtime story. After the story, Sarah said to her mom, "I think my animals and dolls get up and play when I'm asleep." Her mom said, "I don't think they would do that." Sarah decided to look very carefully at her toys before she turned off the light. The next morning she looked at them, and she was sure they had moved.

Story Scavenger Hunt

There are many places where stories can be found. Here are a few ideas:

- ❏ Write a different ending or beginning for a favorite story.
- ❏ Write a fairy tale in which your best friend is a character.
- ❏ Write a silly story about a dog and a cat.
- ❏ Write about a place where everything is the color green.
- ❏ Write a story about a teacher who whispered everything.
- ❏ Pretend you are an ice-cream cone.

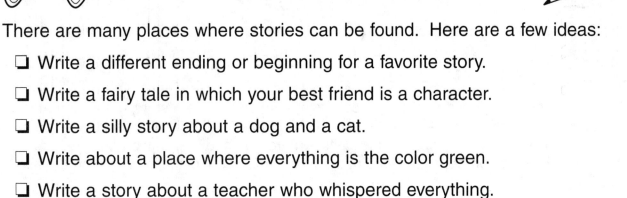

Now see if you can find some story ideas. Write them below.

❏ _____

❏ _____

❏ _____

❏ _____

❏ _____

❏ _____

❏ _____

❏ _____

Chains, Insects, and Clay

Use these creative ideas to motivate your students to produce some very creative writing.

Chain Story

Divide the students into teams of two or three; each team will create a story, one frame at a time. To start, one child chooses a title. The next child provides the first sentence, and so on. Each sentence is written and illustrated on a different frame (index cards work well). When completed, punch holes on opposite sides of the frame and connect them with string or yarn. Hang on the walls.

What If . . . ?

Have students write a short story that tells how things may appear from an insect's point of view. (You may want to read *Two Bad Ants* by Chris Van Allsburg to the class.) For example, what if the student were an ant carrying a crystal of sugar over a kitchen counter? Or what if the student were a flea trying to jump across a puddle in a busy street? The student can change the point of view to almost anything he or she wants—for instance, he or she can write from a dog's point of view or a bear's point of view.

Clay Creatures

Have students create a clay creature using various colors of clay, and then write stories about their creatures! Encourage students to include a beginning, middle, ending, and title for their story. Have students share their stories and describe their clay creatures with a writing partner. Display stories and creatures in the library for all to read and share!

From Doodles to Stories

To increase your creativity, try some modification! Modification is when you take something that already exists and make it into something new by changing it. When you write stories you often take something that is real (your school) and modify it to make a new story (your school as a spaceship). Using the doodles below, draw (or modify) to make the lines into pictures. When you are finished, use one of your pictures as the basis for a story.

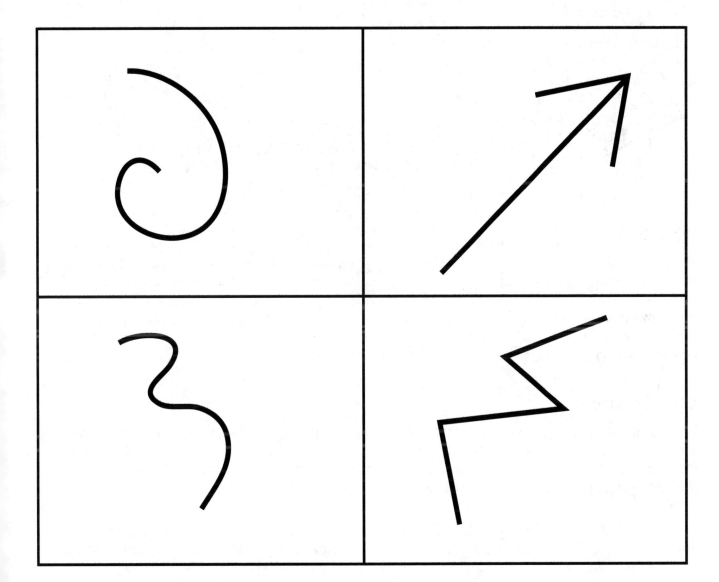

Mysteries, Traveling, and Pictures

The Case of the Missing Words!

Discuss the concept of a "mystery" with your students. Tell them they are going to write a story that has a "mystery twist" to it. They are going to have to leave out certain words from the sentences (words could be spelling words, nouns, adjectives, adverbs). They need to leave a blank line where the mystery words should be. After they write their story, they are to give it to a classmate and the partner reads the story and fills in the blanks with words that he or she feels are appropriate. The mystery story is returned and reread by the author. Is there a new "twist" to their original story idea?

The Traveling Book Club

Here is a fun activity to involve all the classrooms at your grade level. Use large pieces of heavy paper or tagboard and make a blank book of approximately ten pages. Have the first classroom start by choosing a title and making a cover page with title, authors (listing all the classrooms), and illustrators (leave room for these to be added at the end). The blank book is then passed on to the next room. This class decides what will happen on the first page. They write in the sentence(s) and illustrate it. This class then sends it to the next classroom that in turn decides what will happen next. The book continues circulating until it is finished. Share the completed book in each room.

Picture Writing

Find some old magazines and cut out pictures of people and places. Put the people pictures in one envelope and the place pictures in another. Reach into the people envelope and pull out two people (no peeking!). Take one picture from the place envelope. Now take out a piece of paper and make up a story about the people and the place.

Cartoon, Rocks, and Stamps

Sunday Funnies

Direct the students to bring in cartoon strips from the Sunday funnies. Have them eliminate the dialogue by cutting it out or covering it with correction fluid. Tell the students to write a story so that the plot follows the pictures from the cartoon strip.

Mood Rocks

Students create a "mood rock" by finding a flat, round stone and painting a happy face on one side and a sad face on the other. When the rocks are dry, students place their feeling mood rocks on the corner of their desks and write a story in which the character has a happy event happen to him or her, as well as a sad event. Leave mood rocks on desks so students can show how they are feeling daily.

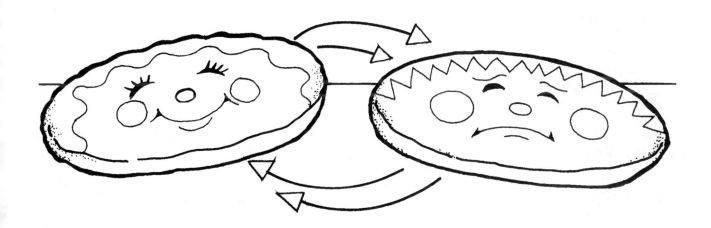

Stamp a Story

Use rubber stamps (or stickers) to create a picture. After your picture is complete, create a story to go with your picture.

Be Creative!

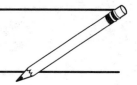

Creative writing needs creative thinking. Here are some ways to be a more creative thinker.

1. **Ask lots of questions:**

   • Why do cats meow?

   • Why is the earth round?

   • How do kites fly?

   • Why do telephones ring?

   • Who invented music?

   Can you think of five more questions?

2. **Ask "what if" questions:**

   • What if dogs could fly?

   • What if snowmen could talk?

   • What if we traded places with our parents?

   • What if none of us had any hair at all?

   • What if we all had to go everywhere on roller blades?

   Ask five more "what if" questions.

3. **Look at the pictures below. For each one, name as many things as you can think of that you could do with each item.** How many can you think of? Just a few? Hundreds? If you want to think of more, try to look at the objects as being whatever size you want and in any position you can imagine. For instance, the box could be a house, a car, a hat, a bed, a dress, a matchbox, a television set, a bus, a building, or a robot if you add a couple of things here and there.

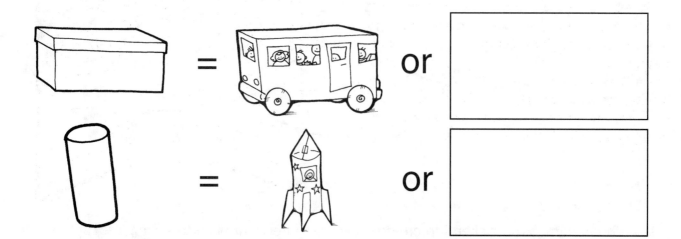

Color, Puzzles, and Magazines

Color Wheel

Make a wheel using a round cardboard disk and spinner; divide the disk into eight sections. Write the name of a different color in each section. For creative writing exercise, have a student spin the spinner—the color it lands on will be the focus for your writing activity.

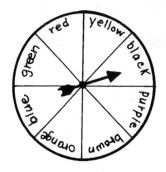

Example:
In the kingdom of red, there was a red castle with rubies and diamonds in the walls . . .

Options for spinning wheel: Use combinations of colors, spelling words, social studies words, science words, "make believe" words, or students' names.

Story Puzzles

Provide a sheet of sturdy paper for each student. Direct them to write a simple story and illustrate it on one side of paper. Then have them cut the paper into 6–8 pieces and mix them up. Allow students to exchange puzzles, put together and read. Give each student an envelope in which to store their puzzle. For extra reading, place the envelopes at the reading center.

Magazine Tales

Have your students fold a regular plain piece of paper into thirds. Provide magazines for students to find three similar (or for a challenge different) pictures. Have them paste the pictures onto the paper. Below the pictures, students will write a simple story that flows from first, to second, to third picture. Have your students give their story a title and share with the class. When all have been shared, collect and stack. Punch holes in the left side and put yarn through to create a big "Magazine Tales" class book.

Mirror Writing

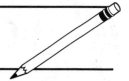

Have you ever tried to write backwards? It is not easy to do. To write backwards completely, making a mirror image, you must write from right to left and reverse the direction of all letters. For example, the word "hello" would be written "olleɥ." In this way, if you held the paper to a mirror, you could read the words clearly.

In the space below, write a letter to a friend, but do so with mirror writing. It seems simple, but it is trickier than it sounds!

I Was So Afraid

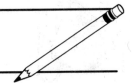

Imagine that you pass by an old house. You hear spooky noises. What's in the house? Would you go inside? On the lines below, write a story about the creepy house. Cut on the dashed lines to make door and window openings. Glue the paper to a sheet of construction paper. Color the picture and draw creatures behind the window shutters and door.

_____

_____

_____

_____

_____

_____

_____

Who Lives Here?

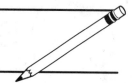

What kinds of things live in caves? Draw a picture of a creature in the cave below. Cut out the cave and glue it to black construction paper. Squeeze dots of glue on the black paper outside the cave. Sprinkle silver glitter on the glue to make stars. Shake off the excess glitter. Write a story about your cave creature and staple it to the picture.

_____

_____

_____

_____

_____

_____

_____

_____

Something Is Under My Bed!

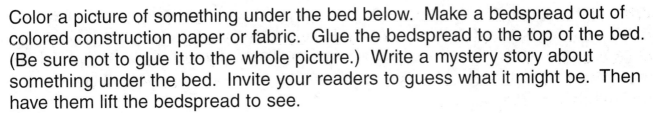

Color a picture of something under the bed below. Make a bedspread out of colored construction paper or fabric. Glue the bedspread to the top of the bed. (Be sure not to glue it to the whole picture.) Write a mystery story about something under the bed. Invite your readers to guess what it might be. Then have them lift the bedspread to see.

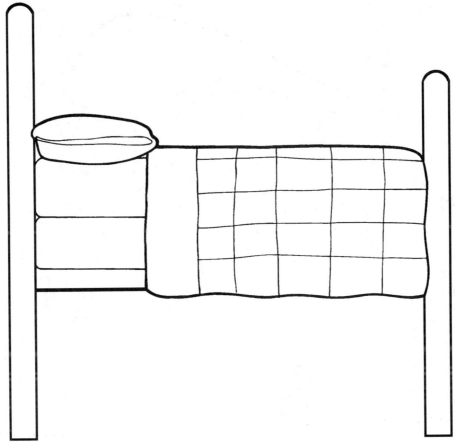

_____

_____

_____

_____

_____

_____

_____

_____

I Imagine . . .

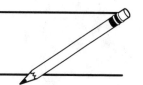

Choose an animal, real or imagined. Draw a picture of the animal you have chosen. Write a story about your animal, including a vivid description of this animal. Read your writing to the class and then ask them to draw the animal as they hear your words. Then, share your picture with your classmates. How do your animals compare?

Magic Wishing Well

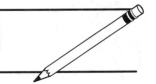

Imagine you come across a magic wishing well. Consider the following questions:

- What wish would you want granted?

- Why do you want it?

- Why would getting your wish make you happy?

- With whom would you share your wish?

- How would your life change with your wish?

Now, write a story on the wishing well about how your wish came true.

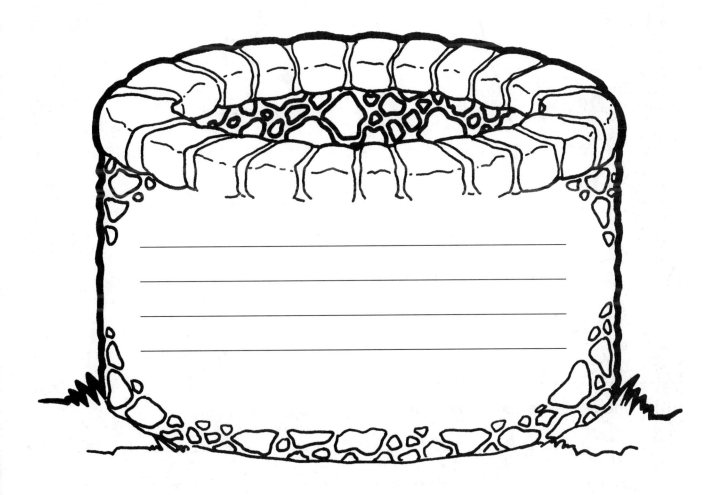

What Is It?

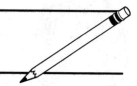

Use your imagination to finish the picture below. Turn your paper any way you wish to help you think of ideas. When your picture is finished, write a story about what you have created. Use the lines below to get you thinking about what you might include in your story.

Write one sentence to explain your drawing.

_____

_____

_____

Write one sentence to explain something your drawing does.

_____

_____

_____

What Did You Dream?

Once I dreamed that there was a castle in my backyard and no one could see it but me. I went inside and found it was full of toys and my favorite foods. I was busy eating marshmallows when my brother woke me up to tell me I was chewing on my pillow!

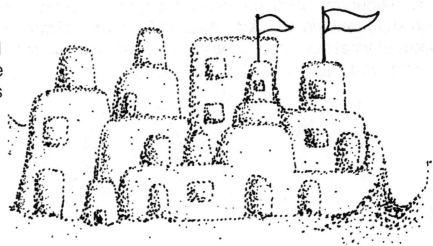

Describe a dream that you once had and draw a picture to go with it.

Mysterious Shapes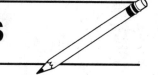

Cut out one or two shapes from page 49. Trace them in the box below. Make each shape into a person, an animal, or an object. Color the picture. Below the box, write a story about the picture.

Mysterious Shapes

What Is That Fluffy Thing?

Glue a cotton ball in the frame below. Use a pencil or crayons to make it into a creature or an object. On the lines below, write a story about your creation.

What's In the Box?

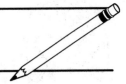

Imagine that you are walking through a park. You find a pretty, wrapped box. There is a note on the box. What does it say? On the lines below, write a story about finding the box and what is inside. Decorate the box when you are finished.

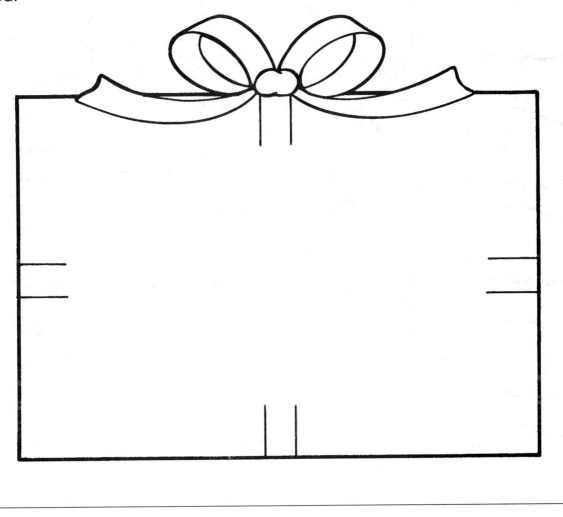

_____

_____

_____

_____

_____

_____

_____

_____

Fairy Tale News

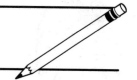

Choose a fairy tale and write a newspaper article about the events that took place in it. Choose a headline from those below (or make up your own) and use the reporter's five W's to tell about the event. Work in groups or as a class to make a newspaper.

Boy Grows Giant Beanstalk!

Prince Charming to Wed

Snow White Wakes Up

Breaking and Entering at Bears' Cottage

Lost Children Return From Woods

Mystery Thief Robs Giant

Letter from Camp

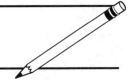

Imagine you have just met one of the characters in your story at a summer camp. You know you are going to become good friends! Write a letter to your parents telling them about your new friend. Be sure to describe his or her physical appearance, reveal something about his or her personality, and relate some camp experience to an event that happened in the story.

_____

Dear _____,

_____

_____

_____

_____

_____

_____

_____

_____

_____

_____

_____

Love,

_____

Advertisement

For Sale

Your parents have given you permission to sell something from your room. In order to do so, you must put an ad in the local newspaper. You must use at least ten words in your ad, but no more than twenty-five words. Your telephone number counts as one of these words.

_____

_____

_____

_____

_____

_____

_____

_____

_____

Literary Valentines

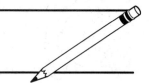

Imagine if Tom Sawyer sent a valentine to Becky Thatcher. What if Nancy Drew sent one to Frank Hardy? What if Clifford the Big Red Dog sent one to Chicken Little? Choose any two characters you know from literature and have one write a valentine to the other. Use only the first names of the two characters and see if your classmates can guess who they are.

My Monster

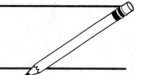

Answer the questions below.

1. Where is your monster hiding? _____

2. What does your monster look like?

_____

_____

3. What does your monster like to do?

_____

_____

4. Is your monster afraid of something? If so, what does it fear?

_____

5. How did you or would you deal with your monster?

_____

_____

Draw your monster here.

Picture Prompts

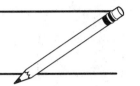

Use the picture on this page to inspire a story.

Picture Prompts

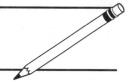

Use the picture on this page to inspire a story.

Picture Prompts

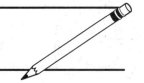

Use the picture on this page to inspire a story.

Box and Hanging Stories

Cereal Stories

Ask parents to help their child cover all four sides of an empty cereal box with brown paper (insides of paper grocery sacks work just fine). Have students bring them to school to use as a creative way to publish their stories.

On the front of the boxes, students will write the titles and draw illustrations suitable for their stories (much like the cover of a book). The story may be written on lined paper and glued to the back side of the box. On one of the narrow sides the author should draw a self-portrait and write about him/herself and family. The remaining narrow side could be used for the dedication, copyright year, and publishing company's name and address. Store the boxes on a classroom shelf. To share these stories, have students select one to take with them to lunch so they can read while they eat.

A Writing Hang Up

Cover wire clothes hangers with black construction paper to simulate tuxedos as pictured below. Have students write and illustrate short stories or poems on white paper to be mounted on the black "tuxedos."

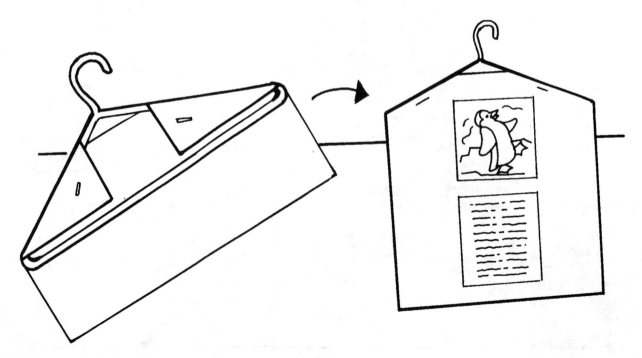

Pop-Up Books

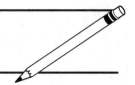

Materials

- white construction paper
- old magazines (optional)
- colored pencils or markers
- glue
- scissors
- crayons

Directions

1. Have students fold a piece of construction paper in half and cut slits down from the fold.

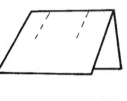

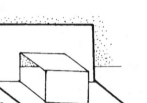

2. Help students push the cut area through the fold and crease it to form a pop-up section. Students can also make a pop-up section by folding a sheet of paper in fourths lengthwise and taping the top and bottom of the paper together to make a rectangular box. Glue the box to the pop-up page.

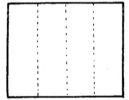

3. Have students make other pop-up pages and glue them back to back.

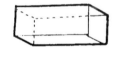

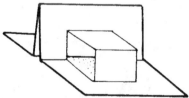

4. Help students write sentences above the pop-up section and glue an appropriate picture from a magazine or drawing to the pop-up page.

5. Help students glue a cover to their pop-up books.

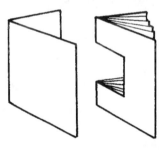

Extension

- Make giant pop-up pages using a large sheet of tagboard.
- Have students glue pictures of themselves to the pop-up sections and write a story called "All About Me."

Pop-Up Variations

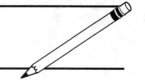

Multiple Pop-Up Books

Multiple pop-up books are excellent activities for stories with more than one main character.

Materials

- construction paper
- colored pencils or markers
- old magazines (optional)
- crayons
- glue
- scissors

Directions

1. Have students fold a sheet of construction paper in half lengthwise.

2. Have students cut several slits down from the fold.

3. Help students push the cut-out sections through the fold and crease them to form the pop-up sections.

4. Direct students to add pictures and text to complete their books as directed on page 61.

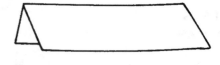

Pop-Up Index Cards

Have students write a question on the index card cover, and write and illustrate the answer on the pop-up section inside.

Filmstrips

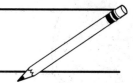

Materials

- 8½" x 11" (22 cm x 28 cm) sheets of white paper
- two 14" x 1" (35 cm x 2.54 cm) wood dowels
- colored pencils
- markers
- cardboard box
- box cutter (for teacher use)
- clear tape
- cassette recorder

Directions

1. Have students write story sentences and illustrations on 8½" x 11" (22 cm x 28 cm) sheets of paper turned lengthwise (landscape). Sentences should be written at the bottom of each page.

2. Help students write the number of each frame in pencil on the back of each sheet. Be sure to include a title frame, credits frame, and an ending frame.

3. Have students read their frames and record them on tape.

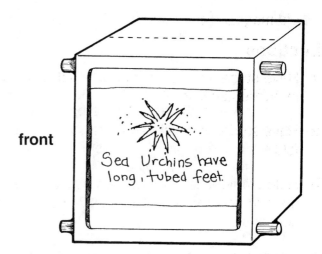

front

4. Help students tape their frames in order from the back with clear tape.

Preparing the Screen

1. Cut an 8½" x 11" (22 cm x 28 cm) hole in the bottom of a cardboard box to make a screen. Make the hole in landscape position.

2. Draw two 1" circles nine inches apart down both sides of the box, and mark an X in each circle.

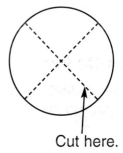

Cut here.

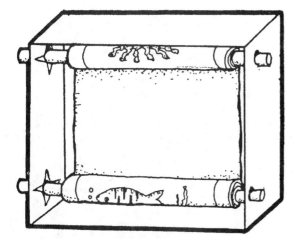

back

3. Cut along each X, and push two dowels through to the opposite side.

4. Help students tape the last frame of the filmstrip to the bottom dowel inside the box.

5. Direct students to roll the filmstrip onto the dowel and tape the first frame to the top dowel.

6. Have students in pairs give filmstrip presentations.

Story Blocks

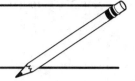

Materials

- tagboard
- colored pencils
- crayons
- markers
- scissors
- glue

Directions

1. Make a tagboard template from the box pattern on page 65 for students to trace and cut out from tagboard.

2. Have students draw in the dashed lines and write "glue here" in the appropriate boxes. Remind students to not write their story nor illustrations on boxes marked "glue here" as they will be covered when the box is finished.

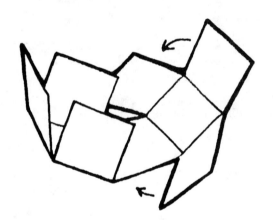

3. Direct students to write story sentences with illustrations on each block face. Have them use one face for their names, the book title, author, publisher, and copyright date.

4. Help students fold and glue their story blocks together by gluing the sides first and the bottom flap last.

5. Display students' story blocks in the classroom.

Extension

Have students put objects inside their story blocks and write a story or description about the object on the story block faces. Let students guess what the object is.

64

Story Blocks

glue here

glue here

bottom flap

glue here

Envelope Books

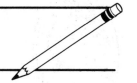

Envelope books provide a fun and creative way for students to be actively engaged in writing.

Materials

- white business envelopes
- paper
- crayons
- colored pencils

- markers
- stapler
- scissors
- tape

Directions

1. Have students stack and staple or tape-bind the envelopes. (See diagram to the right.)

2. Direct students to write sentences and illustrate each envelope page. Remind them that any answers to riddles, math problems, secret messages, etc., will be written on a separate sheet of paper and placed inside of an envelope. An excellent example of an envelope book is *The Jolly Postman* by Janet and Allan Ahlberg (Little, 1986).

Step-by-Step Books

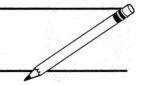

Students can use step-by step books to sequence the events of a story.

Materials

- four 9" x 12" (23 cm x 30 cm) sheets of colored construction paper
- long-arm stapler
- marking pens
- crayons
- colored pencils

Directions

1. Have students place the four sheets of paper on top of one another, overlapping the ends.

2. Direct students to hold the pages together and fold the pages over to create four more overlapping pages.

3. Help students staple the inside fold, and fold the pages back down.

4. Have students write the book title on the top page and write story sentences and illustrations on each succeeding page.

1.

2.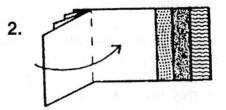

3.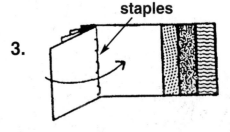

Extension

- Use a step-by-step book to explain how to do something (how to make a cake, how to fly a kite, how to ride a bicycle, etc.)

- Have students keep a diary of one morning's events and write a different time and event on each page.

- Have students write a "time" book with a title like "Eight A.M. in the Lopez Household." On each page have students describe the activities of each family member at that time.

4.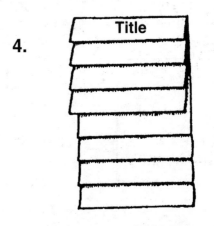

Layered Books

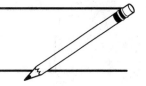

Your students will enjoy making these creative versions of step-by-step books. Pairs can work together to create their own, one-of-a-kind story.

Materials

- colored construction paper
- scissors
- stapler
- markers
- crayons
- colored pencils

Directions

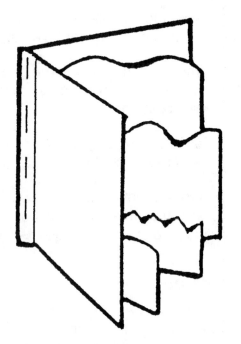

1. Have students fold a large sheet of 11" x 17" (28 cm x 43 cm) construction paper in half to make a book cover.

2. Duplicate the layer patterns on page 69 to create the top edges of each book page. (See diagram to the right for page sizes.)

3. Have students place the pages together with the smallest page on top.

4. Help students put the pages inside the cover and staple along the left side.

5. Have students write sentences and do illustrations on each page.

Extension

- Display the layered books in the classroom without the covers so the layers are visible.

- Teach students about perspective drawing by having them draw foreground, middleground, and background pictures on each layer. Try this technique with ocean, mountain, or forest scenes.

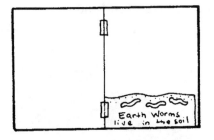

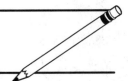

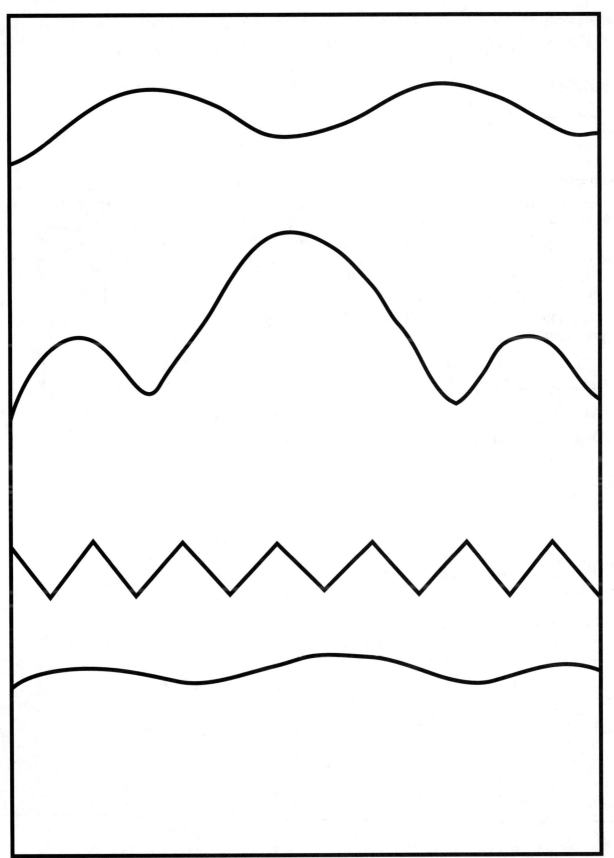

Window Books

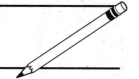

Materials

- construction paper
- stapler
- crayons
- colored pencils
- chalk
- skills knife for teacher use (available in craft stores)

Directions

1. Give each student 8 pieces of 8½" x 11" (22 cm x 28 cm) construction paper, and have them number the pages one to eight.

2. Using the pattern on page 71 as a guide, cut a hole in the size of the circle 1 on the first page, circle 2 on the second, circle 3 on the third, etc. Do not cut a hole on the eighth page of the book.

3. Have students glue or draw a large picture on the eighth page.

4. Help students stack the pages from one to eight so that the smallest window on page one is on top. (See picture.)

5. Have students design a title around the smallest window, and write clues about their pictures on each consecutive window page using descriptive sentences.

6. Help students staple the left side of the pages to complete the book.

7. Have students in pairs try to identify the picture as they turn each page.

Window Books

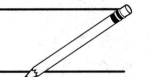

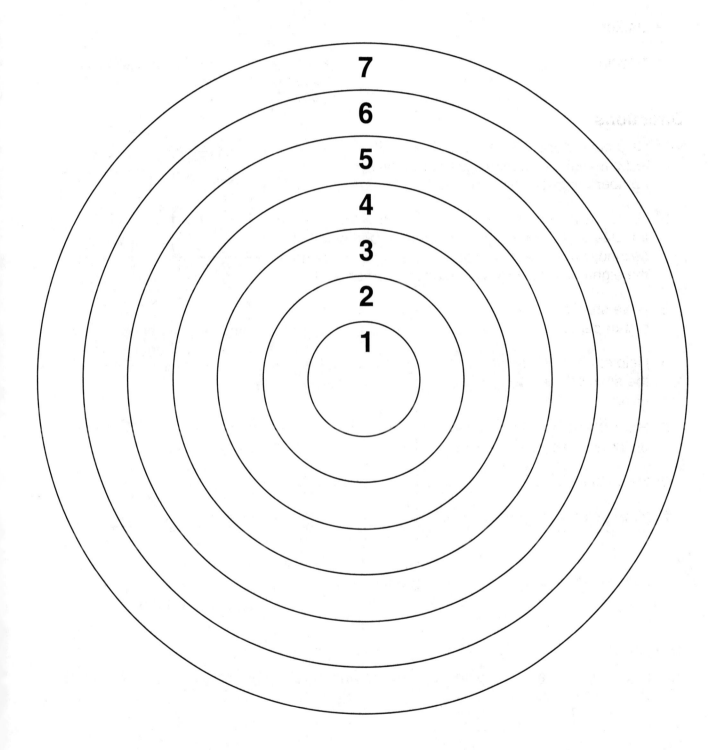

Open-and-Shut Books

Materials

- tagboard
- scissors
- writing paper
- pencils
- fabric or wallpaper scraps
- crayons
- colored pencils
- markers
- stapler
- book tape

Directions

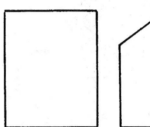
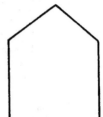

1. Have students cut out two identical pieces of tagboard. (See castle and package patterns on pages 73 and 74.)

2. Direct each student to glue a pattern to one piece of tagboard. This will be the book cover. Students can make a house book by cutting off the corners of the tagboard.

3. Direct students to decorate their book covers and cut the covers down the center on the dashed lines on the pattern. These two pieces will be the "open-and-shut" sections.

4. Help students write stories and staple them to a piece of tagboard cut out in the shape of the pattern.

5. Help students staple and tape the "open-and-shut" pieces to the edges of the back piece of tagboard.

6. Have students in pairs read their books to one another.

Extension

Help students make a fancy castle cover by copying the pattern onto gray paper. Make bricks with white tube frosting.

Open-and-Shut Books

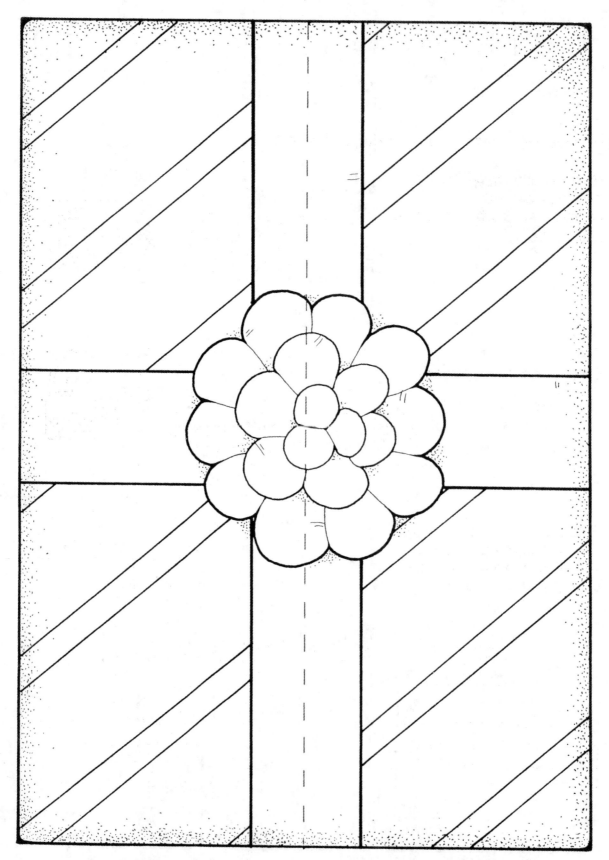

Accordion Book

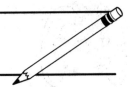

Materials

- white construction or white tagboard paper
- crayons or markers
- pencil
- scissors
- glue

Directions for Friends on the Farm Book

1. Reproduce book covers and writing pages onto white construction or white tagboard paper.

2. Color and cut out pages 76 through 78.

3. Fold Tabs A through F. Glue Tabs A and B together. Glue Tabs C and D together. Glue Tabs E and F together.

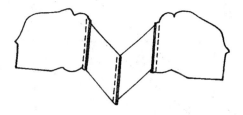

4. Crease each part of the book along the fold lines, forming the book into an accordion shape.

Accordion Book

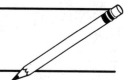

Front Cover

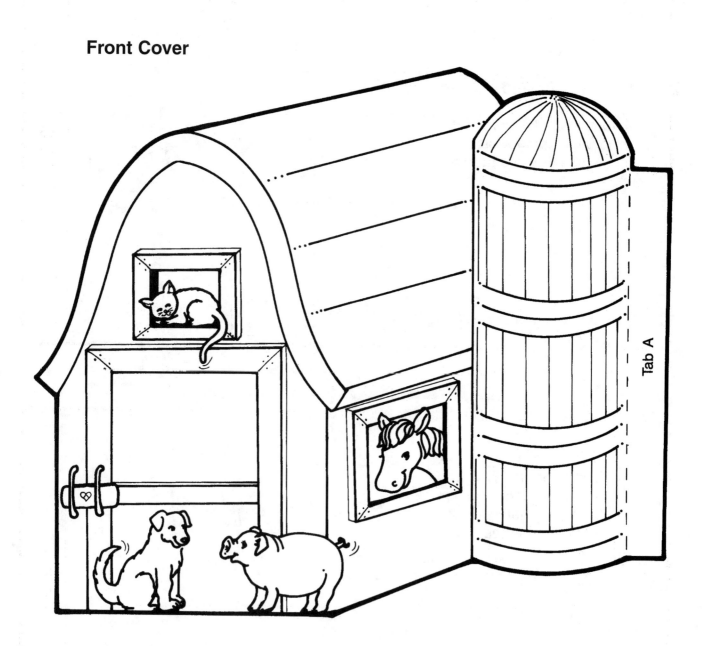

Accordion Book

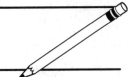

Tab B

_____

_____

_____

_____

_____

Tab C

Inside Pages

Tab D

_____

_____

_____

_____

Tab E

Accordion Book

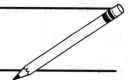

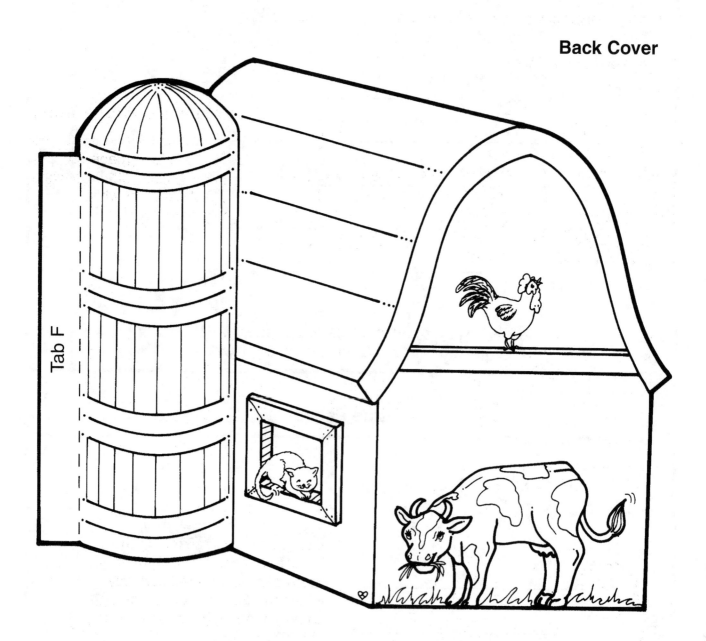

Tab F

78

Wheel Book

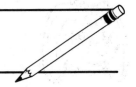

Materials

- white construction or white tagboard paper
- crayons or markers
- pencil
- scissors
- hole punch
- 1 paper fastener

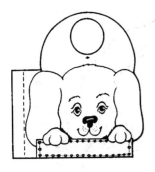

Directions for Puppy Book

1. Reproduce book covers and "wheel" piece (page 80 through page 82) onto white construction or white tagboard paper.

2. Reproduce writing page(s) (page 81) onto regular paper.

3. Color and cut out pages 80 through 82.

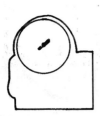

4. Cut out the circle shape on the book's front cover. Attach the wheel behind the front cover by inserting a paper fastener through Dots A and B. The tail tab will help you turn the wheel.

5. Fasten the writing page(s) in between the two covers. Staple or glue the book together on the left side tabs.

Wheel Book

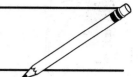

Front Cover

Cut out.

A

My Pet Puppy

Wheel Book

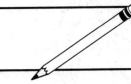

Front Cover Wheel

Inside Page

Wheel Book

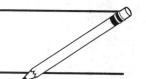

Back Cover

82

Pull-Tab Book

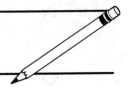

Materials

- white construction or white tagboard paper
- crayons
- markers
- pencil
- scissors
- stapler

Directions for Bird Book

1. Reproduce book covers (pages 84 and 86) and the worm on page 85 onto white construction or white tagboard paper.

2. Reproduce the writing page(s) onto regular paper. (Page 85)

3. Color and cut out pages 84 through 86.

4. Cut the slit on the bottom of the front bird cover. Fold the worm piece Tabs A and B under. Push the worm piece through the slit on the bottom. Unfold Tabs A and B. The worm can now move back and forth along a portion of the ground.

5. Fasten the writing page(s) in between the two covers. Staple or glue the book together on the left side tabs.

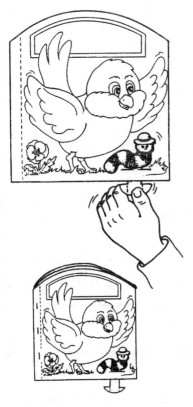

 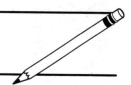

Front Cover

The
Early
Bird

Pull-Tab Book

Inside Page

 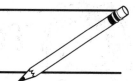

Pull-Tab Book

Back Cover

The shapes on pages 87 through 90 can be photocopied (and enlarged if necessary) for use as shape books.

Themes and Shape Books